I0160765

AZIMUTH OF
GOD

Also by Elizabeth Ayres

Home After Exile:
A Spiritual Odyssey

Mirror of Our Becoming:
Meditations on Nature's Beauty, Wisdom and Mystery

Swimming the River of Stone:
Collected Poems 1966 – 2013

Writing the Wave:
Inspired Rides for Aspiring Writers

Creative Writing from A to Z
(audio book series)

The Ultimate Creative Writing Workshop
(audio book series)

Invitation to Wonder 'Journey' Series
(audio books)

For information on these titles please visit
www.CreativeWritingCenter.com

video recordings of Elizabeth Ayres reading selected poems from this book
are available at
http://creativewritingcenter.com/books/azimuth-of-god

AZIMUTH OF
GOD

*Meditations on
Absence & Presence*

ELIZABETH AYRES

Veriditas
Books

Copyright © 2017 by Elizabeth Ayres

Published by Veriditas Books
P. O. Box 968 • California, MD 20619
301-737-7945
eayres@CreativeWritingCenter.com

All rights reserved. No part of this book may be reproduced, stored in a retrieval system, or transmitted by any means, electronic, mechanical, photocopying, recording, or otherwise, without written permission from the author.

ISBN 13: 978-0-9904258-4-7
ISBN 10: 0-9904258-4-3
Library of Congress Control Number:2016912230

Cover Design by Karen Phillips (www.phillipscovers.com)

for

Mother Aemiliane
and her companions in Christ
at the
Sacred Monastery of St. Nina
in
Union Bridge, Maryland

(Union? Bridge?)

az-ə-məTH

a navigational term
defining the position of a celestial object
with respect to the observer's horizon,
e.g., azimuth of Venus at 47 degrees

from the Arabic, *as-sumūt*, meaning
"the directions" or "the ways"

Contents

Prelude in Four Voices i

Prologue

Syzygy 11

Azimuth of God

Azimuth of God (I) 15
Azimuth of God (II) 19
Azimuth of God (III) 21
Azimuth of God (IV) 25
Azimuth of God (V) 27
Azimuth of God (VI) 29
Azimuth of God (VII) 33
Azimuth of God (VIII) 35
Azimuth of God (IX) 37
Azimuth of God (X) 39
Azimuth of God (XI) 41
Azimuth of God (XII) 45
Azimuth of God (XIII) 47
Azimuth of God (XIV) 49
Azimuth of God (XV) 51
Azimuth of God (XVI) 53
Azimuth of God (XVII) 55
Azimuth of God (XVIII) 57
Azimuth of God (XIX) 59

Epilogue

The Stump 63
The Reef 65

Epilogue (cont'd)

    River & Sky, Their Song of Songs 67
    Migrations 69
    The Heronry 71

Notes 73

Acknowledgments 77

About the Author 79

PRELUDE IN FOUR VOICES

1.

For over two years I have walked with Elizabeth on a spiritual journey that unfolds through, with, and in the lyric meditations of this book. I have tried to affirm for her – and now I'd like to affirm for her readers – how I experienced this poetry as suspended prayer. How it spoke to me of the journey of my own soul. How I walked on the carpet of these words towards that alluring Love which, forever, calls to me. Does that make sense? Let me give you an example.

In the first stanza of "Azimuth of God (X)," I am immediately lifted up by the imagery of the bird, the gull that emerges "from the mist, white feathers glowing/with some hidden, private light." This gull is my soul and I am filled with longing as I streak "towards some conclusion only she can imagine." Do I know where my life is going? Yes, but at the same time, I do not know where my life is headed, we can never know that, can we? So the ache to escape this tension becomes a yearning to fly that propels me into the silent, spaceless nothingness of a mystical flight wherein my soul, like the gull's wings, glows with the energy of God's Spirit. In the second stanza, that reference to Egyptian beliefs reminds me of the universality of the quest every soul must endure as we try to figure out life's meaning. I think I understand, I think I know; but then I realize all my conclusions are just a temporary anchor "beginning/and ending in a shroud/of mystery." I must let go of all my beliefs in order to enter into the transcendent flow of God's Living Light which is also God's Love, a reality beyond human certainty. As I continue to read the words of this poem, deep feelings of love and presence are aroused in me; and at its conclusion, I have been brought to an awareness of God's ineffable mystery which I experience as a "fog," a "low-lying cloud." Yet still I am in flight. Yet still I am searching. Yet still I am me, suspended in Love.

All the poems in this book speak to me in this fashion. In "Azimuth of God (VIII)," I am invited to disappear into a divine beckoning that is part of yet also beyond the natural order: "the slimmest promise/of a door just/a crack, a/long thin glimmer/of light...." In "Azimuth of God

(IX)," I love that line, "The oak has lost its words as well and now it cannot pray." I can rest in that phrase for I and the oak are one. I know that nameless lure. The oak and I remain together in a silence beyond words that is both joyful and sorrowful, a state of pure being where I am suspended, naked, in Love. Truly, it is here, in "night's dark valley" that we meet God "as breath meets flesh and bone."

But you will find your own favorite lines, I'm sure. So I conclude with this prayer: That as you sit with and pass through the words and metaphors of these meditations, you come to know the Peace of God that surpasses all understanding.

– Laura Smith, C.S.J.

Kalamazoo, Michigan
January 2017

2.

I met Elizabeth Ayres by "divine accident." A writing teacher, I was looking for work, searching for a certain school on the Internet, finding hers instead – the Center for Creative Writing. I left a phone message and mailed out a resume. Her call back began a five-year conversation.

In the words of Anne of Green Gables, I'd found a kindred spirit. Both of us writers and teachers, we had that to talk about. And my being a painter, she a poet, each of us struggling for the time to work while making a living – this widened the bond between us. Our conversations were easy, rich, and we agreed to keep talking.

With time the dialogue clarified. Its nature was the spiritual exchange of two artists, Elizabeth beside her river and tall pines, me in my beech and hemlock woods; each of us living the solitary, the contemplative life.

At times we read to each other from various spiritual masters, and we shared our own writing. When Elizabeth began the *Azimuth of God* series, she sent them to me. I read, then struggled to find words with which to comment. The truth is they blew me away. I asked her to read them to me over the phone. The work opened a place in me that is still a struggle to articulate in language, art being its own language, one can only try to point to its impact. The mystery of the work is in the work itself. Try to talk about a Vermeer, or one of Seurat's conte crayon drawings. The mystery is in the artist. The manifestation is from the artist's spirit. My verbal comments were stammered out, trying to express depths the work touched in me. I felt I was in the presence of a singular grace. I knew I was in the presence of art.

"How do you arrive at them?" I asked once. As she described her process it struck me that it was visual, kinetic, it was related to the way I'd describe my own process of painting. It was a kind of painting. I thought. Elizabeth told me she began by free-writing, weeks of it. And walking, body movement, like the Action Painters! The walking let the words she had pushed out move in her, take life. The next phase involved, she said, transferring words and phrases, those that had emerged from her pages of drafting, onto colored papers, using stencil forms. As I listened, I wished I had the medium of film with which to document her movement. I'm glad that I can try to do that here.

My understanding of what happens as Elizabeth works is that words become so detached from the linear mind as to become, not only pure image, but the image of the word itself. Its letters. I connected to her process, which I felt I understood in some intuitive way – I paralleled it to my palette of colors, my brush, as I paint still life, paint objects from life to uncover what is beyond, beneath, around, behind, through the doorway of the objects themselves. The parallel I made was this: Elizabeth's words are like my still life objects, doorways into what cannot be said *with* objects, and cannot be said *without* them.

The image experiences of Elizabeth's Azimuth poems build a ladder to someplace above the earth, a place of understanding which the reader ascends to through the work, rung by rung, word by word, phrase by phrase. Like any great art the work is coherent, takes the reader to a place inside that is whole, and offers a transcendent experience of wholeness to the reader.

The poems are rooted in imagery, highly structured, full of reprise and the way reprise deepens as its contexts change. The Azimuth poems are questions – like Job's to God – and the questions are answered, solidly answered, yet one cannot, beyond the experience of the work itself, say how. It is a superb architecture, crafted by a brilliant poet. It is a vehicle through which a deep spirit can, at last, be set free, like the Sufi's through the whirl of the dervish dance. And that's what I call this *Azimuth of God* series. Dervish poems. Each is a living entity. A full experience. Together they are a learning. An experience of becoming familiar with a place only the spirit can ascend to, and there recognize the truth of its solid reality.

– Helena Clare Pittman

Liberty, New York
January 2017

3.

The divine is often defined as the thing that can be sensed but can never be spoken. God is unutterable. Spirit is unsayable. Light will never be imprisoned in a cage of words. I believed this to be true until I read *Azimuth of God*. Rarely, if ever, has poetry managed to convey so eloquently, so exquisitely, so powerfully, the beatings of my most sacred heart. Somehow, astonishingly, the poems replicate the sensations I experience when immersed in the divine. They give voice to the unspeakable.

The first time I read one of these poems, I found myself transported to another realm. Since then, I've read them multiple times. Each reading unearths another layer of wonder. Elizabeth marries the natural world and the spirit world, the mundane and the sublime, the scientific and the sacred, until all things, all beings, all ways of existing, become holy, touched with her God-centered gaze and attention. I find myself deeply and inexplicably moved by these words, weeping when reading about driftwood, ascending the "black trellis" she imagines being climbed by the stars.

As I have come to know Elizabeth, I have begun to understand the foundation that lies beneath her writings. In "Azimuth of God (IV)," Elizabeth writes, "You will have nothing but some stars/and an unaccountable longing to turn inward/as if unto a great height." Years ago, she rejected her burgeoning career as a poet and dedicated her life to God. She gives her life to contemplation and prayer, choosing to be celibate and solitary in pursuit of a higher truth the stars themselves yearn for.

Elizabeth seems to exist in a plane somewhere between this world and the next. She views her writing as a divine calling, an act of healing for the community that reads her work. Just last year, I had the privilege of staying with Elizabeth for a week in her home on the Potomac River. The moment I walked through the door, I felt the presence of the divine wrap its arms around me. Decorated with icons and sacred images, bathed in sunlight, her home had the peaceful essence of a church. We viewed our time together as a sacred retreat. In the mornings, we observed complete silence, dedicating ourselves to prayer, contemplation, and writing. In the evenings, we came together for a delicious meal Elizabeth had prepared, after which we engaged in corporate prayer, sharing the writings we had produced that day.

Each night, I came to the table with pages of material. Elizabeth, on the other hand, came with a few lines, snatches of God that had come to her during her time of contemplation. Each word was weighed, labored over, vetted. Every mark on the page had been hard-won. Each of the poems in *Azimuth of God* is the product of months of prayer and diligence. Elizabeth reveres the written word. And because of that, every word she writes is imbued with reverence.

As a seeker of truth, a lover of the divine, and a student of the sacred written word, I am honored to have been one of the first to read these poems. The honor is magnified times a thousand now, as I have been chosen to offer them to you, the reader, the person the divine mind imagined when it touched Elizabeth's pen and whispered, "Write this."

– Tawni Waters

Sicily
January 2017

4.

It was sometime in early summer when I first had the privilege of reading *Azimuth of God*. The poet, Elizabeth Ayres, my teacher, mentor, friend, and a wonderful human being, graciously shared a draft with me. I was immediately intrigued by the title. As a lover of language and an avid sailor familiar with celestial navigation, I contemplated the association of the word *azimuth* with the Arabic, *as-sumūt*, meaning, the "directions," or the "ways." And I was excited to discover that *as-sumūt* is indeed the origin of *azimuth*. Such ancient words seem to have larger meanings. In this case, there is a nuance of the three-dimensional. It is not surprising then, the word entered Latin in the context of astronomy, to denote angular measurement in a three-dimensional space. Chaucer was the first to use it in English, in a medieval instruction manual for an extraordinary little navigation device, called an astrolabe, a small, hand-held instrument measuring the inclined position of a celestial body. The device looked like a round locket that opened to reveal multiple flat plates intricately engraved with a kind of mapping to calculate azimuth. I mention these associations about the title, because *Azimuth of God*, in its complexity, its lyrical layers, and rightness of images is like an astrolabe, carefully crafted for the navigators of a particular three-dimensional space: the natural world, the spiritual, and language.

After being dazzled by a first read-through, I was gripped by an inexplicable desire to go outside. In the yard, I noticed a fist-sized rock lodged in one of my trees, a detail I had never noticed before. And at once, I was catapulted back to the poem: "Daily you walk past it, asking yourself/was the boat abandoned in the woods, or did the woods/grow up around a derelict boat?"

And I could not help but think, here is a way poetry is like prayer. In their book, *Poetry and Prayer*, Francesca Bugliani Knox and John Took write that poetry and prayer are "perennial contemplative exercises" practiced through attentiveness. And in her book, *Gravity and Grace*, Simone Weil describes reaping the most meaningful rewards of the human experience through the exercise of attention. She asserts, "Attention, taken to its highest degree, is the same thing as prayer." It has to do with the ability to transform the complex and intermixed world around us into an emotionally and spiritually gratifying form. When it feeds our souls, we instinctively return again and again to a favorite prayer or poem. We may not know how to articulate its mystic hold for us, but we do know how the words, carefully chosen and arranged, make us feel. This is why I feel especially gratified by *Azimuth of God*. In our strained, emotional, and increasingly virtual-reality-oriented times, the attentiveness this work devotes to the natural world – its awe, resiliency, and regeneration – is an ode to the grand mystery of our existence and yearnings. And the graceful language of the poems, like prayer, not only practices attentiveness, but also teaches it.

Azimuth of God seems a culmination of a life's work, a tremendous journey under "nacreous white clouds heaped among indigo molecules," between "ruffled curtains of white surf on a thin brown rod," and "amidst atomic tangos / galactic waltzes." Such lines give me the sensation that, like the rock in my tree, hope and doubt can exist together.

In "Azimuth of God (IV)," the poet inquires, "Is hope a net or is it a web?" If hope is a net, it can be cast; if it is a web, it can simply wait. But does it have to be one or the other?

Perhaps hope is in the questions we ask.

– M. Vanessa Larsen

Boston, Massachusetts
January 2017

Prologue

SYZYGY

1.

The   complex geometry of living the   unforeseen consequence
of light: the branch you so admire for its delicate beauty –

      oval leaves pirouetting on a slender stage of stem – it's

just a shadow   cast by the full moon   shining   behind a branch
and you wonder why it makes you so happy, this
thing that isn't the thing you thought it to be this
sudden apotheosis   of expectation this

2.

syzygy. From the Greek σύζυγος meaning 'yoked together.' A
conjunction or opposition, a   pair of corresponding things. In
poetry, two metrical feet combined into one unit. In

      astronomy, a straight-line configuration of three celestial bodies, e.g.,
      earth, sun and moon. In

         the writings of Carl Jung, the union of opposites within the soul, e.g.,
         yours   on its slender stem   of time, if

3.

you are the one these words are seeking
               as moonlight seeks the lonely branch.

Azimuth of God

Azimuth of God (I)

1.

Sailing from its port of dreams into
leaf-shadows stippling a sun-bright lawn, over
herringbone patterns of wind-ruffled tides, beyond
the coastline of defined purpose and measurable success, finally
relinquishing rudder, compass, map, your heart

curls itself around a question.

If sunflowers bend in yellow adoration of their star;
    if waves rush to the shore's waiting arms;
        if that blind moon strokes earth's face
with the same pale, eager fingers she strokes the raised dots of your life—

where is that toward which all things incline?

        Remember

2.

deep in the woods? The ominous witness of toppled trees, their roots exposed
as too shallow to hold against the storm. Remember

you learned the names of every wildflower edging that ditch? You thought
you could earn your place amidst the planets and the stars. Remember

you walked the beach clutching that rock in your fist? Its cold, smooth
weight seemed like some kind of anchor. Remember,

"God is a circle the circumference of which is nowhere and the center of
which is everywhere." Yes, and

3.

didn't time once stand still?

Didn't the shadows of passing gulls dissolve into wet sand, wind
and wave cease their restless permutations? Yet death

4.

still looms like some forsaken city
in which you left something you cherish.

Standing on a distant hill.

Contemplating those derelict buildings and empty streets
among which you will soon wander.

Envying those nacreous white clouds heaped among indigo molecules
that carry their burdens so lightly.

    Dove of mourning,
    morning's exile, evening's
    pilgrim seeker, why are you saddled with perpetual lament
    while all around you is

5.

jubilation and the trilling song?

The unrehearsed timpani of fireflies in the gloaming.
The pendulous wing beats of herons over wind-ruffled tides.
In herringbone currents, the rhythmic breathing of a moored boat, up
down in
out breath by breath

we receive our life
from beyond time

sail away from our secret ports with such worthwhile dreams toward
such esteemed horizons, the circumference
nowhere, the center
everywhere,
the rudder, the compass, the map relinquished and

don't those shy fish just leap
into your empty
upturned
palms?

Azimuth of God (II)

1.

Daily you walk past it, asking yourself
was the boat abandoned in the woods, or did the woods
grow up around a derelict boat? No

matter. All neglected things tell the same maudlin story:

a hopeful beginning, a progressively complex middle resulting in
a forlorn, forsaken end. No saplings grow
under that crumbling hull, no trees shelter those naked gunnels.

Exposed to the vagaries of an oceanic sky,
the boat rides westward with the white-sailed moon,
toward the horizon's ever-receding and lambent rim.

2.

The salt wave sings its ancient and inexhaustible song.

Sorrow
in the widow's desolate footsteps, the drunk's lonely stagger.
Sorrow
in the murdered corpse's vacant gaze, the killer's satisfied stare.
Sorrow
in history's various illusions masquerading as progress, its
vast loves all clamoring for completion, its
myriad ladders that lead inevitably into exile no matter

your direction, ascending or descending, it's the same
story, an equation you can't quite solve,
an empty swing twisting in the wind and where

has the occupant fled? Ask those two owls
hidden in the pines, trading their ebony secrets.

3.

Ask that saint who said, "God is the immensity in which I lose myself."

4.

Ask that boat on its Godward journey, if you dare.

Azimuth of God (III)

1.

The signs all said
you can't get there from here
but you never gave up searching.

Now, ruffled curtains of white surf on a thin brown rod.
Now, the moon's white thumbprint on a blue blotter.
Now, the white wings of passing gulls, their soprano tremolos.

And one crow, black as night, trapped in these sunshine hours, voice
raw with despair: what we are we cannot know.

2.

The sun creeps from tree to tree stalking its own undoing, hunting
some version of itself yet to be revealed.

Some work yet to be revealed is yours, and yours only.

What we are we cannot know.

3.

If you were a diver.
If you could explore the hidden recesses of desire
where conflicts spread thick as seaweed
where wounds cluster dense as barnacles?

"Deep calls to deep," the psalm says.

What we are we cannot know.

4.

Who is this stranger who walks in your body
among an alien people
speaking no recognizable language?

Time is like sleep, we are lost in it until death
and all dissolving.

Asking ourselves, "How did I get here from there?"

And the river.
Does it envy such things as know

where they begin and where they end?
Oysters in their hard shells.
Crabs with their sharp claws.
Even plankton, safe within the walls of its single cell, but the river —

on a still day

its ruffled curtains thrown open
its glazed window
its blue sky, white moon, gulls, a single crow —

"My me is God," said Catherine of Genoa, "Nor do I recognize
any other me but my God."

5.

The unforgivable sin is

not to ruin your eyes with searching
        in a close and constant darkness;

not to end like a blind beggar
  clutching an empty bowl.

        In this mystery
I find my rest.

Azimuth of God (IV)

1.

"The eye with which I see God," wrote Meister Eckhart,
"Is the same eye with which God sees me." You

think of that great mystic now as you plant pansies
(blue, with yellow eyes) in stone pots, watch

white-sailed boats fly up and down on a blue river watched
by a yellow-eyed sun, but when that bright lid closes

who watches in the dark? The fisherman
has his net. The spider
has her web. You will have nothing

but some stars
and an unaccountable longing to turn inward
as if unto a great height.

    Is hope a net or is it a web?

2.

The mauve rose of early evening has bloomed
and withered on river's trembling stalk; now
the silver hip with its silver seeds falling
on the cold, black ground.

Dogs howling on the opposite shore.

Two owls, their muffled interrogatories.

The big oak, its rustling leaves, its

unaccountable longing to make sense
of these stars tangled in my branches, silver
saplings sprouting up where silver acorns fall.

   Could hope be an eye?

3.

The old words will not suffice to name what blooms and withers
on time's trembling stalk. That which hopes that

which is hoped for the one
desiring the one
desired co-inhering
possibilities observer
and observed all things

crying out their helplessness, their

ache to see as they are seen to know
as they are known to stretch the belly of
infinity's palindrome giving
birth being
born thou

within me I adore thee words
   shooting down from a great dark height thou
within me I adore thee words
   shooting up from a great dark depth thou
within me I adore thee I

of me and I of thee my God we

   adore.

Azimuth of God (V)

1.

On its two great wings of ebb and flow, the river alights upon the shore.
Sings to your soul, "Arise! Take to the sky

of your belonging, its branches blue, its clouds heavy as ripe fruit,
arise now, go and eat your fill."

2.

When you were a child, perhaps you knew how to tie a boat to a pier, how
to make your knots secure, perhaps

you have forgotten, perhaps your knots no longer hold, perhaps you

envy the knots of others but how, so bound, could you sail?
The mauve blossoms of the crepe myrtle gush from its fountain mouth.
Go now, quench your thirst.

3.

Between storm and storm, where does the thunder hide?

With two great wings of birth and death you arrived on time's green shore.

Wondering where you came from.
Wondering where you're going.
Wondering where to find refuge
between storm and storm.

4.

If pressed to say something about time, would you
point to a ticking clock? Summon
memory's bumbling apprentice, history? Its
slapstick antics of finitude, its
burlesque mimes of eternity.

Two great wings.
Storm after storm.

5.

In emerald boats cicadas sail away on waves of sound.
Ebbing and flowing the waves of sound

"Arise!" sings night to dusk. "Go!"
sings day to dawn. No mistaking

invitations issued by
an unseen, unknown, unanswering yet felt
source. No mistaking

the cost of
yes,
the price of
no.

Two great wings.
Crest and trough.

Azimuth of God (VI)

1.

Between lamentation and hallelujah
between strife and jubilee
between what you've done
and what's been done to you
if only

there were a door just
the slimmest promise
of a door just
a crack, a
long thin glimmer
of light could you would you
disappear?

Uncurling from its spool of moonlight
the silver river wraps
around the silver shore.

Self after self you gave yourself
to death layer
by shining layer unspooling
from what shining core?

High above, clouds flutter:
the lost wings of silver birds.

If it's not a tragedy
of unspeakable complexity
what is it?

You navigate the ragged coastline
of trust and betrayal. Vectors,
velocities, a shifting wind

spills the brimming chalice
of a purple morning glory
into a purple-starved world.

Perhaps it's a species of flower.

2.

The eagle's cry scrapes the air
like a rusty hinge. Back
and forth the seasons swing

on a rusty hinge. Trust,
betrayal, what you've done, what's
been done to you. The damaged pine

oozes sap layer by bitter fragrant layer

obliterates the wound. Seven times
seven bitter fragrant times
you forgive. Perhaps

it's what Beatrice showed Dante: love
that moves the sun and stars.

3.

Dawn, that suspect soothsayer.
Twilight, that oracular crone.
Standing vigil at your door proffering

their chalice. The spider pours
shining silk from her shining core.
Lamentation. Hallelujah. The spider's egg sac

cracks and spills. Strife. Jubilee.
Small birds with miniscule hungers appear
then disappear. The silver river's silver waves

fill the silver shore. High above, shining clouds
obliterate the shining moon

light brimming over
into a light-starved world.

And what about those bees,
working the surprised blossom
of your open mouth?

Azimuth of God (VII)

1.

At dawn these still waters were filled with clamoring gulls.
Now, in morning's languid light, just the harsh contralto

of a journeying crow, the muted bass and treble of waves
from a passing boat's wake. Tall pines on the opposite shore

cast long, green reflections onto the motionless river, making
(you think) a long, green road boasting many unmarked

entrances and exits, many signs in strange languages you
almost remember, many vaguely familiar landmarks and

fleeting faces almost recognizable as beloved, but once

you mistook a monarch butterfly for a falling leaf, unable
or unwilling to distinguish between surrender and free flight.

2.

The hurricane turns out to sea, or back upon the huddled city.

Paused between push and pull on a long green road. Prepared

for opposite outcomes, the aftertaste of trial and error bitter
in your mouth. Where do shadows go in the dark? If the work

of light is to give itself to that which it is not, what is the work
of God? Moving forward cautiously, an oarsman through fog.

Not that it's unknowable, mystery, but that it can be infinitely
known. *For the rest of my life*, said Einstein, *I'll ask myself,*

What is light? Or the Augustinian friar Walter Hilton: *The soul feeleth well there is somewhat above itself that it knoweth not*

nor hath not yet, but it would have it, and yearneth for it burningly. Or St. Mechtild of Magdeburg, to whom the Beloved said,

You have the wings of longing, you know the pull of hope, so why not soar into the blissful heights where I await your love?

3.

The stuff of their making unmakes them. Such is the work of God.

4.

In the throbbing chest of the throbbing year, light expands and light contracts. The work of God is the heartbeat of God, a throbbing

bass and treble of visible and invisible. What you knoweth not, what you burn to know. Pushed and pulled on this long green road

of forgetting and unforgetting, its hidden points of access, its mysterious signs, landmarks of dubious recall, faces, shadows,

butterflies, leaves, what matter
if you fly or fall?

Azimuth of God (VIII)

1.

You cannot see the wind, invisible above it; nor the current,
invisible below, but what's revealed
of wind and current on the river's surface, this

you can see—a trembling jigsaw

of light and shade. Like sticks
in a nest, the white gull thinks, and where

are my eggs? Her wings make question marks
as she rises, flying into the open sentence
of her perplexity.

2.

He died in autumn, when the fiery petals of marigolds
combust, their acrid scent clinging to the flesh like smoke.
Autumn. When green leaves reveal their fiery secrets,
and fraying threads of light unravel

to the selvedge. Is death
life's unyielding limit? Will unseen threads
continue to unravel? All you know

in your house perched beside the abyss, all

you seem to know is that twilight erases
what dawn restores. Tears of grief and tears
of joy, your seesaw ache of loss and gain—a

trembling jigsaw—sticks

in a nest. Or maybe

3.

he died in some other season. Maybe he's
a she. Maybe

4.

you are the one rising

in an uncertain season

perplexed by your new and fiery name—
Theotokos, God-

bearer, divine birth-
giver, God
from God, light
from light, true God from true God

begotten not made

one in being with

all that is seen and unseen—sticks

in a nest or

5.

wings?

Azimuth of God (IX)

1.

In bleak mid-winter the river wakes. Never mind the ice,
she thinks, how is it I never knew
such stillness could be mine? Above,

the wings of gulls roil the frigid air. Below,
the fins of fish churn the frigid mud. Within,

some kind of night
gnaws at some kind of moon, eats it down
to the bone.

2.

The road before you soon becomes the road behind.
You march in place, getting nowhere, no

where? The road
in front now

here the road
behind. Watchman,

what of the night? Watchman,
what of the night? Night

comes and morning follows. Within
thick clouds, a flock of geese, their cries
of ardent longing for a destination

unknowable except in the going.

3.

Night cannot cloak the old oak's shame, its
lost leaves its
barren branches its

misplaced grief for the outworn semblance of a former self.

"I am going to lure her, and lead her out into the desert. There
I will speak to her heart." Night

comes, and morning follows. Wherever
there are no signposts, that is the desert, now
here now

there those geese

flying north or flying south
according to some nameless lure.

4.

The oak has lost its words as well and now it cannot pray.

5.

Who is this coming up from night's dark valley? There
I awakened you, O my people, in the stillness

beyond words

here

I will meet you

as breath meets flesh and bone.

Azimuth of God (X)

1.

Out of silence into story the gull emerged
    from the mist, white feathers glowing
        with some hidden, private light.

As I said, it took me aback. No
    river, no sky, no shoreline, just
        gray fog then that lone white bird

streaking toward some conclusion only she could imagine. It

2.

makes you wonder, doesn't it? The ancient Egyptians believed that in
addition to the physical body, a person is made up of parts that together
constitute the individual: *ren*, the name; *shuyet*, the shadow, *ka*, the life-force;
ba, the soul; *akh*, the spirit. Egyptian funerary religion is devoted to ensuring
the survival of the body with all its components, but as I said,

3.

that mist, dense as time, beginning
    and ending in a shroud
        of mystery, you and me

streaking through it, trying to hold on to all our parts. Did you know

4.

fog is made up of condensed water droplets, the result of air being cooled to
the point where it can no longer hold all of the water vapor it contains. Fog is

a low-lying cloud, its moisture generated locally, as from a nearby body of
water, as from

5.

a corpse
     cooling
          after the last breath. Now

there's a story, wouldn't you say?
     You and me emerging
          on time's far side? Scientists

6.

say light is emitted in tiny packets called photons that travel through space
exhibiting properties of both waves and particles. It's a paradox, a
fundamental property of the universe, they say. The name, the shadow, the
life-force, the soul, the spirit, maybe they're words, maybe they're something
else. In

7.

the beginning was the Word, and the Word
     was with God, and the Word
          was God, as

8.

I said, out
     of story into

Azimuth of God (XI)

1.

Whitecaps on the river, tight white fists raised against the wind.

Whitecaps on the river, a school of fish harried by the wind.

Whitecaps on the river, a flock of birds flying into or out of, from
or towards, if only you could know for sure, the wind,

the way it bends the branches of leafless trees, the way they
plead with it, the way
you plead with it,

time, counting your remaining minutes
while the river does a strange math—

the westering sun's fiery digit points east
across the waves—

the beginning, not the end, of the journey.

2.

Long tall pines press long tall shadows onto the melting snow.
The quiet light swoons into evening's eager arms.

Geography's secret counsel—everything

given nothing
held back everything
received nothing
rejected.

3.

Is the universe a flower or is it
a bird? Are these petals unfolding or wings

unfurled? Into or out of, from
or towards, if only you could know for sure, in

the beginning …

4.

a formless void … darkness over the deep … potentiality and power … God
said … seed, egg, a fiery flash … time unfolding, space unfurling … God
said … gravity, electromagnetism … God said … energy, particles … God
said … heating, cooling, expanding, contracting … a billion years, a billion
galaxies, a billion billion stars … everything given, nothing held back …
orbiting planets, a billion billion living cells … beginning, ending, beginning
again … everything received, nothing rejected … 13.7 billion years …
whitecaps on the river, long tall pines, the spirit of God fills the whole world
and that which holds all things together

5.

knows every word.

6.

The quiet light curls itself into evening's arms.

Two owls outside your door, hidden
in the pines, their
antiphonal chant, their

questions of escalating urgency—who

am I reaching for, who
is reaching for me? From

and towards, flower
and bird, a

strange math, a

single fiery digit—

beginning and end, whole
beneath the whole of who you are.

Azimuth of God (XII)

1.

$\qquad$ Where, amidst
pale corpses $\qquad$ of wildflowers on a frozen beach $\qquad$ dry sticks
jagged shells $\qquad$ sand $\qquad$ spilling from cracks in driftwood like
marrow $\qquad$ from cracked bones,
$\qquad$ where

is love? Ice
clings to the old pier's pilings, every shivering wave
striving
to tether itself to something solid. What

is love? Early and late $\qquad$ shadows
ring out across the land $\qquad$ heralding
time's comings and goings $\qquad$ who

will come to heal the wounds of winter? Don't say
spring, for every season suffers. Who, amidst
atomic tangos $\qquad$ galactic waltzes $\qquad$ who

$\qquad$ will heal your seasons?

2.

The salt spray, the stiff wind, the wings of gulls like whitecaps on a
darkly swollen river $\qquad$ of clouds. Many voices $\qquad$ ringing out
as one voice, defying $\qquad$ multiplicity, defying $\qquad$ finitude

defying life itself, for mustn't love transcend
all strivings and seasons? The

sticks and shells and shadows   *yh*
the blooming stars and shining flowers   *vh*
ever on your lips   *yh*
tethered to your breath   *vh*

> *YH VH*
>   *YH VH*
>   *YH VH*

Azimuth of God (XIII)

1.

The bottom of a bottomless well can only be a falling.

2.

Does the river find herself on every swelling tide?
Or does she lose herself again and again, not even caring
that she is lost?

      Emptying
and filling on your own dark tides.

      Embracing
perplexity like that star
swerving across the sky, its

incandescent its paradoxical
smile.

      Falling, falling.

3.

Multiplied by infinity, every desire swerves back on itself to become
love's cipher. Don't ask
why, ask

where, e.g., that roadside ditch
swollen with rainwater. Looking down

into those still depths, you discover
long tall pines thrusting up, a
blue sky, a
shivering breeze. Every

green needle trembles, trembles, every
green droplet falls, falls, every concentric ring stirs
the water's surface—
    up meets down
    above meets below
    paradox meets perplexity
but don't ask where, ask

why, e.g., that
suicide bomber in his vest, trembling, that
old man in the rubble, falling, that
loud-mouthed, fear-
mongering politician, stirring

the water's surface, desire
multiplied by infinity. Love's
bottomless well. If

it's anywhere, it must be

everywhere. "Deep

calls to deep," the psalm says, a
luminous abyss calls out
to an abyss of darkness, light

like a tide, emptying, filling, and you

not caring if you're lost or found.

Azimuth of God (XIV)

1.

Waxing moon in a daytime sky—
what blue bird watches
with this pale white eye? Every

curling wave a lifted wing, every
feathered pine bough flapping, all
the hollow bones of all
the hidden stars—

wherefrom this need to fly, whereto
this soaring?

2.

Moses said, "Show me your glory," and God replied, "I will hide you in the
cleft of this rock as my glory passes by, for you cannot see my face and live."
Hidden

in the rocks between thus and so, obstacles
appearing out of nowhere to thwart
your every desire. Can

boats dream? If
boats dream, what about
this one, upturned
on its lonely spit of sand, hull
shattered, stern
splintered, barnacles
obliterating the name—
a sharp Braille spelling out some other name, perhaps, or
a map to some far and glorious shore? "You

cannot see God's face and live," says the boat, its glance
borrowed from eternity, its promise
extracted from your demise. You

shake your head and walk away but that blue bird
still keeps vigil. Your
beating heart. Your
feathered breath. Your
bones.

3.

Moses said, "Show me your glory," and God replied, "I will make all my
goodness pass before you and proclaim to you my name, but my face you
cannot see." Lost

in pleated folds of hope and despair. It's not
the bars of light and shade on a
sun-streaked beach that keep you caged, it's

all your whys and wherefores. See that gull
stalled by the wind? See that gull
pivot
on thermals? See that gull
soar
on currents she cannot see? A

sharp and glorious Braille of
yes and yes and yes and yes of
     yes and yes and yes and yes of
          yes and

Azimuth of God (XV)

1.

Because they fly and are not birds, you love them.

Because they trace an erratic route through time's wordless green avenues.

Because they bear the burden of myth, and are maligned for it.

Because, amidst all those songs named
and unnamed, arranged
and erupting – frogs

    croaking in their soggy vernal ditches, stars
    keening beyond season in their black gullies – the bat

taught you what legs and arms are for. Remember? Catching fireflies

in glass jars to make lanterns of their dying? You knew it
even then: the gift
and the sacrifice thereof are one and the same soaring. As

Jesus knew it on his cross. Arms flung wide
as wings he keened, "My God, why
did you abandon me?" Or that fish—

    carried aloft in the osprey's sharp talons, torn
    by the osprey's sharp beak, high up
    in the oak tree now and privy

to the mysteries of flight.

2.

       Other things
you might put in a jar: that
solitude you are trying to avoid, that
inner emptiness. But how else

illumine the route? In their underwater caves
don't blind fish grope through albino darkness
that is as light to them? Don't fireflies ravage night
with the mythic brilliance of their yearning? You

3.

died a thousand times to get here. Why not
remember it as song?

Azimuth of God (XVI)

1.

Thunder, that troubled bird, perches on a jagged bough. Clouds
thick as leaves. Bursts of light. What strange fruit, that

blooms
ripens
rots

in a single instant.

2.

Odin climbed the cosmic tree, Yggdrasil, that grew from what deep roots?

Nine long days and nine long nights above the holy well he hung, pierced
by his own spear. God
to God given, they say, self
given to self. All for the sake
of mystery's alphabet. And don't you

refuse to learn the names of constellations? Let them
speak their own mystery, you think, let me
speak mine through them; when river opens her dark arms

to the morning sun, sparkling bangles at her wrists—
not gold not silver not diamonds not any word
in any language I could know this side of death.

Is time a keg that empties and fills or is it
a well?

Don't we all have our spears?

3.

Every storm brings a wind that does not know the light
yet parts the charcoal leaves to expose light's fruit. You

bloom　　　ripen　　　rot　　　seed　　　root

in some far country remembered from a dream. Not
north not south not east not west not any direction you can fix

on your compass. Ululating ribbons
of wild geese twine
about your branches, this

constellation no one can name.

Azimuth of God (XVII)

1.

Whenever she opens her wings the hawk discovers flight.

Could it be that easy?
         As it folds
and unfolds through the seasons, just to rise up

on the light? Soaring

above the house where grief lives
the house with the door that will not close. Crying out

         "Love! Love!"
all day and into the night. Ascending

on pure gravity now, on
paradox

to fathom the life of things, of
conditionality and necessity, of

hope   despair   doubt   consent   fear   trust

questions like thin fingers on the keyboard of time, this
chiaroscuro of tumbling notes, this
chord.

2.

The magnolia's white moons sail
across their green sky. On its golden red stem
the setting sun blooms. What else could it be but love, this

life of the life of things? *Oh!* she cried out,

       Trinity whom I adore!
My three, my all, my beatitude, immensity
in which I lose myself! Between two pier pilings
a spider's web shines; between two stars
energy and matter darkly strung; between two wings
flight

that immense net

   in which you are

     released

     and held?

Azimuth of God (XVIII)

1.

Clouds heaped like oyster shells
on a blue beach.

Stars like roses climbing
on a black trellis.

And the river.

>   While you lie sleeping the river
dreams for you: falling freely
from a steep, rocky cliff. Don't you know

this geometry yet? How
all inhabitants of time's flat plane
yearn for infinity's vertical? While you lie sleeping the pine

sends deep roots through earth's dark seas to find you.

2.

The dove regards the fallen world and sighs, her trembling heart
the witness—

>   love always eclipses
whatever desire aroused it.

3.

Perhaps, tomorrow, you will wake.
Perhaps, tomorrow, on some deserted beach you'll find

oyster shells pale as clouds, or flowers flung
thick as stars and shining with a cool, distant light. Your geometry

will collapse. Your
points and lines. Your
questions of shape, size, identity, position answered by

little white boat-birds flying
through blue water with
sharply pointed wings. Up

and out, those V-shaped sails. Down
and in, those V-shaped reflections, those

glistening diamonds

in your blue, your trembling
heart.

Azimuth of God (XIX)

Dawn. The sun

summons crimson snakes from river's dark basket. You

wake, heart
writhing, flesh
like the banks of some river.

Those birds. And light
trilling like a flock of birds, galaxies crooning
the pinwheel notes of their song. Vast numbers

with many zeros stretch from there to here, treble
of shine, bass
of shade, your

heart, its
unheard descant, its

pinwheel flight.

Midnight. The moon

slices through an onyx river, her silver fin flashing. In
every owl's yellow eyes the sun
rises, sifting shadows
for their secrets. Even in sleep your heart

    caught   consumed   transfigured

wakes, gazing at all things
from within all things
where there are no things just

that river, its
currents of shine and shade.

                         Dawn. The sun

rises as the moon sets. And time

like a fast boat

skimming river's surface.

EPILOGUE

THE STUMP

I remember you. You stopped, admiring
what they have done to me, these waves, with their unrelenting
ebb and flow. Me,

my roots so deep, I thought myself
secure, but impossible to defend against the encroaching river, its
abrasive upsurge, its scouring

downrush. Me. Bereft
of bark, sap, limbs, leaves, all a tree should do and be; me,
worthless, disintegrating

to splinters but you
oohed and aahed over my remnant form, bent down, stroked
the rough swirls, the

corrugated eddies where
pith and core had been. "You look just like a wave," you sighed, and
I felt it, a surge within.

You walked on; I remain
with the waves, their mantra of perpetual longing mine now, mine
their endless flow.

THE REEF

We call to them but they do not hear us, adrift forever
in the somnolent tides of that lofty black river.

       Some among us believe
they are free-swimming larvae, and tell their children, "This
year, to this reef, the travelers will come home." Others think

they are pearls, and mourn the fate of those
who toiled ceaselessly yet passed without witnessing
the glory wrought from their pain. Still others hold

we were created in their image; are meant
to join them when we die, meant to shine.

       I share
the opinion of the few: we abide here
and there simultaneously, as firmly fixed to that reef
as to this; and

    the voice with which we call to them is
their voice, timelessly given, perpetually shared; and

    if they seem not to hear, it's because

gazing at us they see

       not oysters, only stars.

River & Sky, Their Song of Songs

Drifting in his serene blue currents, white stones form
and reform. Like me, they are undone by his glance.

> In her shining blue eyes, I see myself reflected.
> The loom that wove her, wove me.

His very touch transfigures. The scales of fishes turn to
feathers; with them I ripple, I swell, I soar upwards
seeking my lover.

> Hypnotized by my lover's beauty, the birds of the air forget
> how to fly; with them I swim, blind, in her looking-glass realm.

At times, his gray despair suffuses me.

> When she is downhearted, I cannot find myself.

Beyond that cerulean exterior, the landscape of his dark and endless core
reveals me.

> Underneath that azure surface, her black and fathomless canyons
> explain me.

Set me as a sun in your highest arch,
    a wave on your farthest shore.
No storm can drive love away,
    nor can ice immobilize it.
For potent as the first singularity is love,
    vigorous as gravity its devotion.

MIGRATIONS

Out of nowhere the urge was upon me, sharp as a beak. Berries
still green on the vine. Cones
still green on the pine's
lofty bough, now
this. Flying

into the open maw
of a devouring need.

I think I knew it all along. One day I would climb
this blue and corkscrew ladder
and not look back —
flecks of egg shell littering the nest. That recurring nightmare
of confinement. And those crows, their black bodies
like shovels digging crow-shaped tunnels of egress into

what? Oblivion? Eternity? I had to learn

and the leaves, flapping their wings in the wind,
straining their beaks in a single direction. From?
Towards? Within

the cloud rain
doesn't know itself
as rain

everything
pecks at its shell, even stars,
those halting configurations of fire on fire. "Do this

in memory of me," your holy man said, and it wasn't the lure
of foreign shores, now was it?

Body, blood, soul, divinity, I tunnel into
the unsteady air, a God-shaped configuration
of hope and fear. Do this

in memory of me.
And the joyful singing everywhere.

The Heronry

In late winter they abjure their vocations to solitude, their empty brown
beaches, their jagged black jetties, their silent green tides that ebb and flow

endlessly. The great blue herons assemble in the tall, thin air at the tops of the
pines, where winds swell like a green river, where trees sway in a green tide

endlessly. Pair by pair, the herons build their nests. Stick by stick, hundreds
of herons build their nests, lay their eggs, the generations ebbing and flowing

endlessly. Let us, then, for this little while.

For the sake of what's to come.

In the swelling winds of want, in the green tides of plenty.

In this tall, thin air and
word by word:
a nest.

The sky, too, has great, blue wings, and endlessly;

we huddle beneath that blue breast.

NOTES

"Azimuth I" – "God is a circle the circumference of which is nowhere and the center of which is everywhere." Used contemporarily by Thomas Merton, the phrase goes back at least as far as the pre-Socratic poet and philosopher Empedocles. It's been variously attributed to St. Augustine, St. Bonaventure, St. Thomas Aquinas, Meister Eckhart, Nicholas of Cusa and other mystical writers.

"Azimuth II" – "God is the immensity in which I lose myself." This line is adapted from the journals of St. Elizabeth of the Trinity, who actually said, "The Blessed Trinity is the immensity in which I lose myself."

"Azimuth III" – "Deep calls to deep" appears in Psalm 42:7. The conclusion of this poem was informed by a reading of Johan Baptist Metz' spiritual classic, *Poverty of Spirit*.

"Azimuth IV" – In Section 3, "to know/as they are known" paraphrases 1 Corinthians 13:12, "Now we see only an indistinct image in a mirror, but then we will be face to face. Now what I know is incomplete, but then I will know fully, even as I have been fully known." The phrase, "Thou within me I adore thee" is quoted from *Christophany: The Fullness of Man* by Raimon Panikkar (Orbis Books 2004).

"Azimuth V" – The phrase "unseen, unknown, unanswering yet felt/source" is adapted from William Maxwell's testimonial to Robert Lax which appears on the back cover of Lax' *33 Poems*. (New Directions, 1988). The actual quote, in context, reads, "I don't know any religious writing that moves me as much or is as persuasive as the prose communication with the unseen, unknown, unanswering but felt fountain-source of his belief, which begins: "Searching for you, but if there's no one, what am I searching for? Still you…"

"Azimuth VI" – The phrase "seven times/seven times" echoes the Gospel of Matthew 18:21-22. "Then Peter came and said to Him, 'Lord, how often shall my brother sin against me and I forgive him? Up to seven times?' Jesus said to him, "I do not say to you, up to seven times, but up to seventy times seven." The end of the section alludes to the last line of *The Divine Comedy*, which is "The love that moves the sun and the other stars."

"Azimuth VII" – The lines "Not that it's unknowable, mystery, but that it can be infinitely/known" are adapted from Richard Rohr, who said, "Mystery is not unknowable, it is infinitely knowable."

"Azimuth VIII" – In addition to its literal meaning, "God-bearer," the word "Theotokos" is traditionally used to refer to the Mary, the Mother of God. Lines in that stanza and in the following two stanzas are excerpted and paraphrased from the Nicene Creed, which begins, "I believe in one God, the Father almighty, maker of heaven and earth, of all things visible and invisible. I believe in one Lord Jesus Christ, the Only Begotten Son of God, born of the Father before all ages. God from God, Light from Light, true God from true God, begotten, not made, consubstantial with the Father; through him all things were made...."

"Azimuth IX" – Section 2 alludes to Isaiah 21:11-12, "Watchman, how much longer the night? Watchman, how much longer the night? The watchman replies, 'Morning has come, and again night. If you will ask, ask; come back again.'" Section 3 paraphrases Hosea 2:14: "So I will allure her; I will lead her into the desert and speak to her heart." Section 4 alludes to the Song of Songs 8:5: "Who is this coming up from the desert leaning on her beloved? Beneath the apple tree I awakened you; there your mother was in labor with you, there she was in labor and gave you birth." This section also alludes to Ezekiel 37:1-14, a passage called "The Valley of Dry Bones."

"Azimuth X" – I'm indebted to Sanchita Balachandran for the explanation of Egyptian beliefs found in Section 2. The wording is paraphrased from her paper "Among the Dead and Their Possessions: A Conservator's Role in the Death, Life and Afterlife of Human Remains and Their Associated Objects," *Journal of the American Institute for Conservation*, Vol. 48, No. 3 (2009): 197-219.

"Azimuth XI" – Section 4 alludes to the Genesis account of creation and to evolutionary theory, especially the Big Bang and its aftermath. The words that end that section and flow into Section 5 ("the spirit of God fills the whole world and that which holds all things together//knows every word") are from The Book of Wisdom 1:7. In Section 6, the phrase "whole beneath the whole of who you are" is from Ilia Delio's book, *The Unbearable Wholeness of Being: God, Evolution and the Power of Love* (Orbis Books 2013).

"Azimuth XII" – For the use of YHVH as a breath prayer in Section 2, I'm indebted to Richard Rohr who cites it in his lecture at Norwich Cathedral, "Becoming Stillness." The lecture is on YouTube at https://www.youtube.com/watch?v=9TGS-JD80nE. YH and VH are the only Hebrew consonants that do not allow the speaker to use the tongue or close the lips. The Hebrew name for God, YHVH, is thus a replication of breath, *yh* on the in-breath, *vh* on the out-breath. Also see Richard Rohr's book, *The Naked Now: Learning to See as the Mystics See* (Crossroad 2015), Chapter Two, "The Great Unsaying."

"Azimuth XIV" –Sections 2 and 3 allude to Moses' encounter with God as related in Exodus 33:18.

"Azimuth XVI" – Section 2 alludes to a story concerning the Norse god, Odin, who lived with the other gods in the upper branches of the world tree, Yggdrasil. At the roots of this tree was The Holy Well of Urd, where the Norns had hidden the runes ("mystery's alphabet") until Odin sacrificed himself to obtain them.

"Azimuth XVII" – There are two allusions in Section 1 which deserve attribution. The phrase "to fathom the life of things, of/conditionality and necessity" comes from Martin Buber. The complete quote reads, "When you fathom the life of things and of conditionality, you reach the indissoluble; when you dispute the life of things and of conditionality, you wind up before the nothing; when you consecrate life, you encounter the living God." The pairing of doubt and consent, fear and trust was inspired by a passage in Martin Laird's *A Sunlit Absence: Silence, Awareness and Contemplation* (New York: Oxford University Press, 2011). The relevant quote is: "This luminous, flowing Vastness is constantly present whether we turn our gaze within or without, for in this Vastness there is no within versus without. This ground-awareness does not joust with divine presence-versus-absence, for it embraces both. It is beyond any possibility of doubt, for awareness saturates both doubt and consent, and its silence embraces both fear and trust. It is as Teflon to both past and future. Untouched by time, but without being excluded by time, it is yet within time but without being contained by time. Too simple to come and go, it is the 'fullness of time.'" In Section 2, the lines "Trinity whom I adore!/My three, my all, my beatitude, immensity/in which I lose myself!" are from the journals of Elizabeth of the Trinity.

"**Migrations**" – The phrase "Do this in memory of me" was spoken by Christ at the Last Supper and, when spoken by a priest at Mass, refers to the act of consecrating bread and wine such that they are transubstantiated – their substance changes from bread to the "body, blood, soul and divinity" of Jesus Christ.

Acknowledgments

It's been said that prayer happens when the truth of who we are encounters the truth of who God is. Since such a meeting is beyond human devising, I begin by acknowledging God, who initiated the encounter these words hopefully express.

I always knew the poems were prayer for *me*, but I couldn't have known they were prayer for others without the ongoing support of the four women whose voices comprise the prelude to this book. Laura Smith, C.S.J. has been a wise and compassionate spiritual guide for many years. Helena Clare Pittman's friendship and depth of spiritual vision has been one of my greatest consolations. Tawni Waters' sensitive and heartfelt readings were a source of courage. M. Vanessa Larsen's insightful and articulate responses convinced me that a broad spectrum of truth-seekers could find hope in these words.

Support comes in many ways, of course. I would never have been able to finish this book without the loving presence of dear friends in my life: Jane Sypher, Kellie Gofus, Jim Walsh, Theresa Prymuszewski, Janaki Patrik and Jan Booth. Nor could I confidently have made this book public without the editing assistance of Stacia M. Fleegal and Janice Booth.

Finally, I'd like to thank Burlesque Press for publishing "Syzygy," "The Heronry" and "The Reef." OnBeing.org published my essays "The Circle Dance" (which includes "Syzygy") and "A Passion for Place" (which includes "The Reef" and "The Stump").

About the Author

Elizabeth Ayres is the author of four previous books and the founder of the Center for Creative Writing, which is now being ably directed by poet Stacia M. Fleegal. The Center's website is www.CreativeWritingCenter.com

Elizabeth currently lives in Tall Timbers, Maryland, where Herring Creek meets the Potomac River, which meets the Chesapeake Bay, which meets the Atlantic Ocean, which meets the Pacific Ocean, which meets the Indian Ocean and all other seas. The world is a vast round ball, every place touching every other place, all of it touching God.

www.ingramcontent.com/pod-product-compliance
Lightning Source LLC
Chambersburg PA
CBHW021347090426
42742CB00008B/768

9 780990 425847